A World of Homes

LEVEL 6

Written by: Nicole Taylor
Series Editor: Melanie Williams

Pearson Education Limited
Edinburgh Gate, Harlow,
Essex CM20 2JE, England
and Associated Companies throughout the world.

ISBN: 978-1-4082-8816-0

This edition first published by Pearson Education Ltd 2013
10
Text copyright © Pearson Education Ltd 2013

The moral rights of the author have been asserted
in accordance with the Copyright Designs and Patents Act 1988

Set in 15/19pt OT Fiendstar
Printed in Great Britain by Ashford Colour Press Ltd.
SWTC/01

Acknowledgements

The publisher would like to thank the following for their kind permission to reproduce their photographs:
(Key: b-bottom; c-centre; l-left; r-right; t-top)

Alamy Images: Alistair Laming 39 (a), Andry A / Alamsyah 8b, Arcaid Images 11b, Arctic Photo 8t, Aurora Photos 3 (igloo), 7t, 39 (g), Caro 11tr, 16cr, 30b, Caroline Eastwood 12tr, Chris Howes / Wild Places Photography 36t, Clynt Garnham Architecture 16tl, Construction Photography 30t, Cro Magnon 9b, Danita Delimont 17br, david speight 19br, David Wall 26br, DesignPics Inc 4c, Kathy deWitt 15t, Elizabeth Whiting & Associates 32cl, 39 (c), Fancy 23tr, Franck Fotos 20b, Gerner Thomsen 6t, Horizon International Images Limited 25bc, Iain Masterton 19l, Ilene MacDonald 29t, Imagestate Media Partners Limited - Impact Photos 5b, 25tc, incamerastock 32cr, Independent Picture Service 10bl, Janusz Gniadek 21t, Jeff Morgan 05 15b, Jochen Tack 18r, Joe Vogan 3br, 27t, Johner Images 4b, JTB Media Creation, Inc 37b, Marion Bull 14l, Mathias Beinling 18cl, Matthew Taylor 3 (tent), 6b, Neil Cameron 25br, 39 (b), John Norman 10br, Prisma Bildagentur AG 27b, Rob Cousins 34t, Robert Fried 9t, 39 (e), Stock Connection Blue 3bl, 20cr, Timothy Swope 39 (d), Tips Images / Tips Italia Sria Socio Unico 22b, Tom Mackie 16br, Travel Stock Collection-Homer Sykes 35l, travelib prime 16cl, Wendy Kay 12b, Adriadne Van Zandbergen 10t; **Architects Senosiain:** 21b; **Corbis:** Eric Robert / Sygma 20tl, Jonathan Blair 26cl, Michael Patrick O'Leary 25t, Nik Wheeler 9cr, Kazuyoshi Nomachi 22, Ralf-Finn Hestoft 33t; **DK Images:** Barnabas Kindersley 7b, James Brunker / Rough Guides 5t, Kim Taylor 24r, Martin Richardson / Rough Guides 28t, Nigel Hicks 17t, 17c; **Getty Images:** Echo 34b, sot 31t; **Nice Architects:** 29b; **Photo Courtesy of Justin Sailor:** 28b; **Shutterstock.com:** art&design 23c, Becky Stares 13t, Iwona Grodzka 14cr, Kamira 37t, Stuart Monk 35r, 39 (f); **Tham & Videgard Arkitekteer; Tree Hotel in Harads, Sweden:** Ake E:son Lindman 28cl; **View Pictures Ltd:** James Brittain 33b

Cover images: *Front:* **Alamy Images:** Kathy deWitt

All other images © Pearson Education

In some instances we have been unable to trace the owners of copyright material,
and we would appreciate any information that would enable us to do so.

Illustrations: Mark Ruffle

For a complete list of the titles available in the Pearson English Kids Readers series, please go to www.pearsonenglishkidsreaders.com. Alternatively, write to your local Pearson Education office or to Pearson English Readers Marketing Department, Pearson Education, Edinburgh Gate, Harlow, Essex CM20 2JE, England.

Contents

What is a Home?

Why do we need homes?

We need homes to protect us from the weather. The roof and walls protect us against the sun, rain, wind and snow. Homes help keep us warm in winter and cool in summer.

Houses can protect people from attack by their enemies, thieves or wild animals. People keep things that are important to them inside their homes.

Homes make life more comfortable. They are a private place for families. Furniture like beds, chairs and tables makes life easier.

Homes in history

Today most of us live in houses or blocks of flats. Many people live in villages, towns or cities but a long time ago most people round the world were nomads. This means that they travelled from place to place. They made homes that they could take with them. When the seasons changed, they explored new environments to find food for themselves and for their animals.

When people learned to grow food and to farm animals they needed to stay in one place. Because they did not need to move, they built permanent homes.

Nomads today

Life as a nomad is often difficult and sometimes dangerous. In the modern world it is easier and more comfortable to stay in one place, but some people are still nomads today.

The Nenets travel with their animals over the large spaces of Siberia. They carry their homes with them. They make them from animal skin and wood.

tent

Some Bedouin people are still nomads. They travel across North Africa and The Middle East with their animals. They live in tents that protect them from the sun, wind and the cold nights.

The Inuit live in the Arctic. There are no trees or plants where they live. They eat fish and sometimes whales and other animals. In winter, some Inuit people still make houses from the snow. These are called igloos. The ice walls and roof protect them from the cold.

There are still a lot of nomads in Mongolia. Mongolia is a very big country and the nomads need to move during the year to find food for their animals. They live in round houses made of wool and wood. These are called gers.

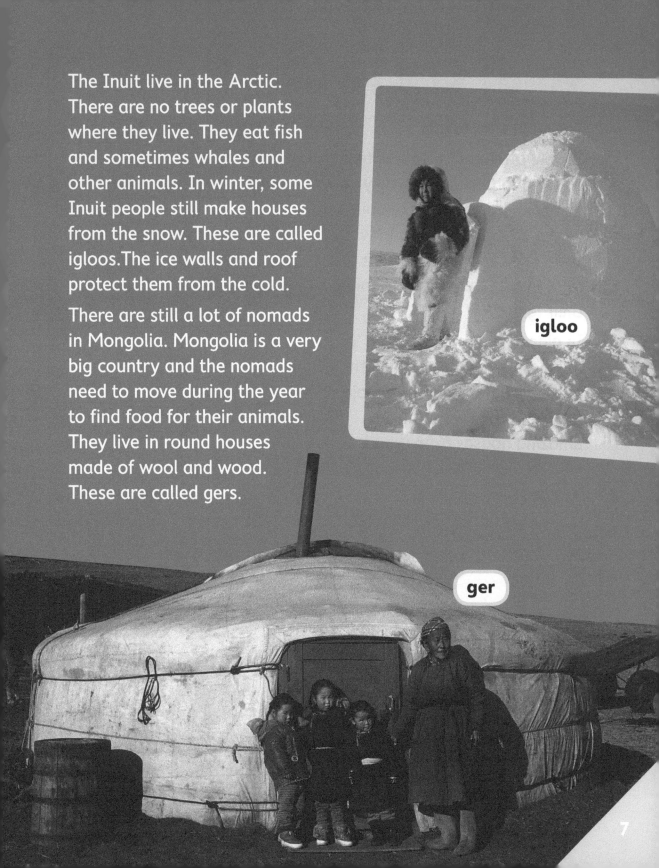

igloo

ger

What are Homes Made of?

Natural materials

People often make houses from building materials that they can find round them, for example, wood, stone, or plants. In winter there is a lot of snow where the Inuit live so they use it to make their igloos.

In places where there are a lot of trees, people often build their houses from wood. The Toraja people in Indonesia make amazing houses from wood.

Did you know?
There is an ice hotel in Norway. There are ice walls, an ice roof and even ice beds!

In some parts of Asia, people use bamboo for building. Bamboo is light and very strong. It is one of the fastest growing plants in the world.

Did you know?
In some places bamboo can grow up to 100cm in 24 hours.

In places where there are rivers or lakes, people sometimes use reeds to build their houses. Reed houses can be large and very beautiful.

Stone is a very popular building material. Stone houses are very strong. They protect people from the wind and bad weather. If there is a fire, stone walls do not burn.

Earth and bricks

In many countries people build their houses out of earth. When it is wet, earth is easy to use and you can make it into a lot of different shapes. This earth house in Mali is large.

You can dry earth and make it into bricks. Bricks are very hard and they make a building very strong. Brick houses can be tall. In Yemen there are some very beautiful earth and brick houses.

It is easy to move bricks to different places. People do not always need to use the same materials. They can use bricks, too.

brick

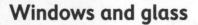

Windows and glass

The Romans were some of the first people to use glass for windows. Glass windows let the light in but keep the rain and wind out. In China and Japan, before there was glass, people sometimes made windows out of paper. Three hundred years ago, making glass windows was difficult and expensive. In Britain only rich people had glass windows. Many houses were very dark inside. Now glass is much easier and cheaper to make and most people have glass windows. Some houses even have glass walls.

Did you know?
Glass is made of sand.

Concrete buildings

A lot of builders use concrete to build with. Concrete is a mix of materials. These materials change when you mix them with water. They become very hard when they dry. You can make concrete into different shapes when it is  wet. The Romans used concrete to build some of their most amazing buildings. Hadrian's Pantheon is two thousand years old. It has one of the largest concrete roofs in the world. After the Roman Empire ended, builders did not use concrete very much again until the nineteenth century.

concrete

Do you live in a block of flats?

Modern cities have a lot of concrete buildings. Concrete buildings can be very tall and have a lot of floors. Architects often choose concrete to build blocks of flats because it is very strong. Flats are like houses but there are many of them in one building. A lot of families can live in a block of flats. In very tall blocks, there are lifts to take you up and down.

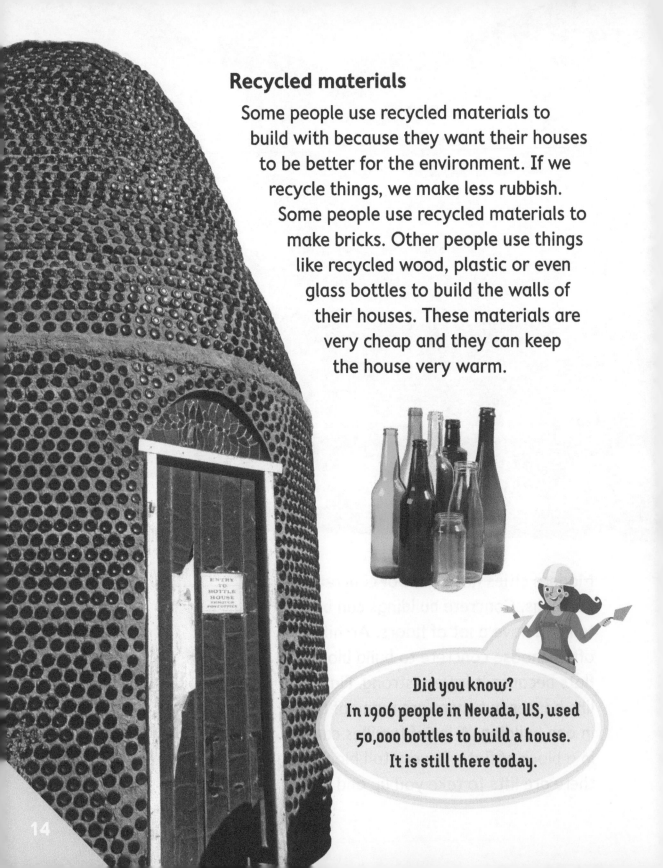

Recycled materials

Some people use recycled materials to build with because they want their houses to be better for the environment. If we recycle things, we make less rubbish. Some people use recycled materials to make bricks. Other people use things like recycled wood, plastic or even glass bottles to build the walls of their houses. These materials are very cheap and they can keep the house very warm.

ENTRY
TO
BOTTLE
HOUSE

Did you know?
In 1906 people in Nevada, US, used 50,000 bottles to build a house. It is still there today.

14

Some architects design houses from unusual things, for example, containers from ships. These containers are very quick to put into place and make into small blocks of flats. They use less energy and fewer materials than building a new house.

Straw is another good building material. It is cheap, light and quick to build walls with. The builders cover the straw with earth to keep it dry. Straw walls are thick so they stop the house from getting cold in winter and they keep it cool in summer.

The Shape of Homes

Roofs

Houses in cold countries often have sloping roofs to protect them from rain or snow.

In countries where there is not much rain, a lot of houses have got flat roofs. In some very hot countries, houses have rounded roofs. This shape helps to keep the house cool because the hot air goes to the top of the roof.

In the past, some houses in Iceland had earth and grass on the roof to protect them from the cold and wind. In the jungle, some houses have a roof but no walls. This lets the fresh air in.

stilts

Stilts

In some countries, houses have stilts. These stilts keep the house dry and people can keep their animals under the house.

Some fishing villages are on stilts over the water. The families can keep their fishing boats near their homes and there is no danger if the water rises.

People who live in forests or jungles sometimes build their houses up in the trees. This protects them from wild animals and insects. The houses are very high up so they can see a long way.

Have you ever been in a treehouse?

17

Skyscrapers

As cities get bigger, the land to build on gets more expensive. It is cheaper to build tall buildings with a lot of floors. Many modern cities have a lot of very tall buildings. These are called skyscrapers.

People started to build skyscrapers at the end of the nineteenth century. One of the first famous skyscrapers was the Empire State Building in New York. One of the tallest buildings in the world today is the Burj Khalifa in Dubai. It is 828 metres tall and it has 163 floors. There is a hotel in it too.

Small homes

Homes can be very small. For example, in big cities like Tokyo, many families live in small flats. This is because there are a lot of people in the city and there is not much space. Some architects now design very small houses because they use a lot less energy, materials and space. They are much cheaper to build than big houses and they are better for the environment too.

Did you know?
The smallest house in Britain is less than six square metres.

Strange homes

With modern materials people can explore new ideas for buildings and their shapes. Today architects often choose metal and glass to make interesting shapes and some of them are amazing.

Some people like to make their houses look different just for fun. The house above is very unusual. The windows and doors are round. It has a swimming pool. It must be fun to live in.

Look at this house.
What does it look like?

Did you know?
In the US there is a house that looks like a shoe.

In Poland there is a house that is upside down. The roof is on the ground and the floor is in the air. The rooms are upside down and the furniture is too! A lot of people go to see it. It was very difficult to build and it is impossible to live in it.

There is a house in Mexico called the Nautilus House. Living in this house is like living inside a sea animal. Inside it is very colourful and light. Everything is round and there are no corners.

Which house would you like to live in?

Inside Homes

Decoration

People like to decorate the inside of their homes. Decoration tells us a lot about the people who live in the house. More than 15,000 years ago, people painted pictures on the walls of their cave homes. They painted with earth and plants. The pictures were often of people and animals.

In South Africa the women of the Ndebele people paint colourful designs in the rooms and on the walls of their homes. These designs belong to their family. The women pass the design on to their daughters who paint the designs in their own way.

Many people like to change the design and colour of the rooms in their homes. They use paper or paint to cover the walls and they choose furniture that they like. Some people like designs and decoration from the past. Other people prefer very modern designs.

Young people often decorate their rooms with pictures of famous people and things that they like. Some people like to decorate the walls with photos of their friends and family.

Do you have any pictures in your room?

Rooms in a home

Some homes have only got one room for sleeping and eating. Other homes have got different rooms for different purposes. For example, there is a kitchen for cooking, a bedroom for sleeping and a bathroom for washing. In flats, these rooms are all on one floor. In houses there are two or more floors joined by stairs. Some houses have got a room at the top, under the roof, called the attic. Other houses have a room under the house called the cellar.

attic

cellar

How many rooms are there in your home?

24

Furniture

In some countries people like to have chairs and sofas to sit on. In other parts of the world people prefer to sit on carpets on the floor. A bed is a very important piece of furniture in cold countries.

In some hot countries people prefer to sleep in hammocks because it is cooler. People in Central America were the first to use hammocks over 1000 years ago. When you are not sleeping, you can easily put the hammock away to make space.

Have you ever slept in a hammock?

Homes of the Past, Present and Future

Cave homes

Before people built houses, they often lived in caves. In a cave, the temperature does not change very much. When it was cold outside, the cave was warm. When it was very hot outside, the cave felt cool.

In some countries, for example Turkey, people made houses in the rock. People still live in these houses today.

In Coober Pedy in Australia, people live in underground houses. In Australia, it can be very hot but these houses stay cool. There is even an underground church.

Earth houses

In the past, people sometimes built houses into the side of a hill. A part of the house was underground.
There was earth and grass on the roof. This protected the house from fire, wind and cold. This was very important in cold countries like Iceland.

Today, architects are using the same idea to build interesting houses that save energy. These houses are often called earth houses.
In Switzerland there is a small village of earth houses. Some of these houses have doors in the roof. They are easy to keep warm.

Old ideas, new houses

Here are two different treehouses. One is in the jungle and it is made of natural materials. The other one is a modern treehouse made of glass. You can see the trees round it but you cannot see the house.

teepee house

Some Native Americans lived in tents called teepees. Teepees had a hole at the top for the smoke from the fire. Here is a modern teepee house. It uses the same teepee shape but it is made of stronger material. There is no hole for the smoke but light comes in through the top.

Mobile homes

Some families live in motor homes. They can drive their home from place to place. Some people do this to look for work. Other people live in motor homes because they enjoy travelling.

This modern mobile home uses energy from the sun and wind to keep it warm. You can use a car to move the house. Two or three people can live in it.

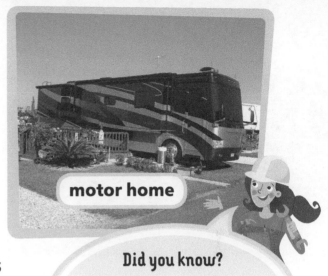

motor home

Did you know?
Motor homes can be very expensive and bigger than some houses!

'Green' homes

It is important for homes of the future to use clean energy. For example, more houses will use energy from the sun and the wind. They will use water from the rain and recycle the water from the bathroom and kitchen.

There are some new houses that go round in a circle. This means that the house moves with the sun. In winter, the windows point to the sun and the sun keeps the house warm all day. In summer, the house turns away from the sun. In this way it does not get too hot.

Intelligent homes

In the future houses will be 'intelligent'. A computer will open and close doors and windows. The lights will turn on when you walk into a room and turn off when you go out. The temperature inside the house will change when the weather changes outside. The computer will even water the plants when you are on holiday.

It is possible that future cities will be on the sea. These cities may be like large leaves on the water. If a lot of people live in cities on the sea, this will save space on land.

Unusual Homes

Making changes

It is popular today for people to make their homes out of other buildings. For example, people have changed old schools, shops and factories into houses. In Britain there are some old windmills that are now people's homes.

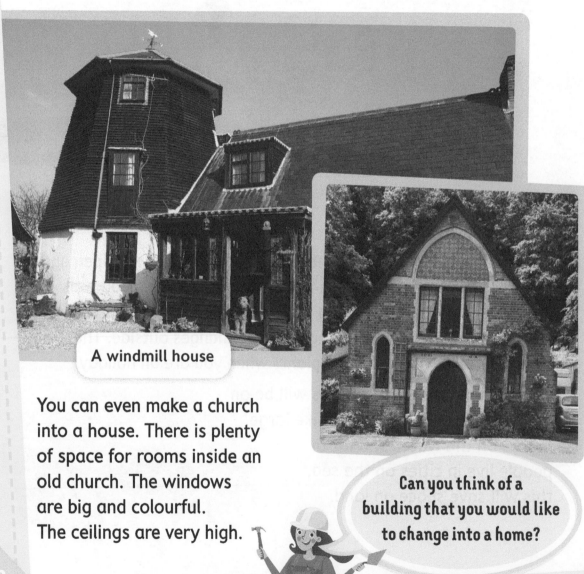

A windmill house

You can even make a church into a house. There is plenty of space for rooms inside an old church. The windows are big and colourful. The ceilings are very high.

Can you think of a building that you would like to change into a home?

Some people even change planes into homes. They take out the passenger seats and put in bedrooms, bathrooms and kitchens. If you live on a plane, you have a lot of windows. But you cannot fly the plane!

Other people make houses out of old trains, buses or lorries. A train house is very long and narrow. It has a lot of windows on both sides so it is very bright inside. A bus can have two floors so you can have bedrooms on the top floor. A lorry has got a lot of space at the back to make rooms.

A train house

Houseboats

Another unusual place to live is on the water in a boat or a houseboat. Narrow boats are boats that travel slowly on the water. They take materials from city to city, like a lorry. Some narrow boats are still working boats today. The workers live inside the boat. Some people make narrow boats into homes or holiday homes. They can move from place to place like nomads.

Some houseboats are very big and do not move at all. These are more like a house than a boat. Others can sail round the world and are very comfortable inside.

houseboat

Lighthouses

Lighthouses are on the coast, on islands or on rocks. At night, they have strong lights that tell ships of danger. In the past, they were also people's homes. Sometimes life in a lighthouse was very difficult. If the lighthouse was on an island out at sea, the person who lived there was often alone for months and months. Today most lighthouses work by computer and no-one lives in them. Some people buy old lighthouses to make into homes. The rooms are round and have no corners. They have got a lot of stairs!

Are there any castles
in your country?

Castles

In the past, important families lived in castles. The castle protected them against their enemies. Castles had high, strong walls made of stone. They were often high up on a hill and you could see for a long way. Some castles had water all round them to make it difficult for enemies to attack.

There are still some amazing castles round the world today. A lot of them are museums now.

Palaces

A palace is a very big and very comfortable house. Rich, important people like kings and queens live in palaces. Inside, they are often very colourful. They have got very expensive materials and furniture. There are often large gardens, lakes or forests round them.

Buckingham Palace in London has got 240 bedrooms and 78 bathrooms! The Palace of Versailles in France has got 700 rooms and 2,153 windows.

palace

Which house in this book would you prefer to live in?

Glossary

architect (n) page 13   a person who draws the plans for a building

block of flats (n) page 5   a big building with a lot of homes in it

builder (n) page 12   a person who makes houses and other buildings

building materials (n) page 8   things which people use to build houses, for example, bricks, bamboo, wood

decorate (v) page 22   to make something look nice with colours or pictures

mobile home (n) page 29   a home that can move from place to place

nomads (n) page 5   people who do not live in just one place. They move their home from place to place

skyscraper (n) page 18   a very, very tall building

Before You Read

❶ Work on your own or with a friend. Make a list of materials that you can use to build a house. Now look for them in the book.

❷ Match the words and pictures.

> windmill   bamboo   hammock   skyscraper
> houseboat   igloo   lighthouse

When you have finished, find the things in the book and write the page number. Have a competition with your friends. Who finished first?

After You Read

① **Do the Book Quiz.**
You have one minute to choose the correct answer
for each question. Check your answers in the book.

a Which of these things can you NOT make a house of?

1	bottles	**4**	ice
2	bamboo	**5**	rubbish
3	water	**6**	animal skin

b In rainy countries it is better to have

1	no roof	**3**	a flat roof
2	a sloping roof	**4**	a roof with a hole in it

c A skyscraper has got

1	one floor	**3**	no walls
2	two floors	**4**	a lot of floors

d Which of these homes cannot move?

1	a ger	**4**	a tent
2	a teepee	**5**	a cave
3	a motor home	**6**	a houseboat

② **Look through the book. Which is your favourite home in the book? Tell your friend why you like it.**